PEANUT BUTTER

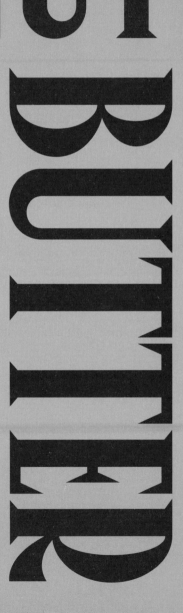

Breakfast
Lunch
Dinner
Midnight

Tim Lannan
& James Annabel

PEANUT BUTTER

Breakfast
Lunch
Dinner
Midnight

Tim Lannan &
James Annabel

Hardie Grant

BOOKS

DO YOU LOVE PEANUT BUTTER?

(NO)

Really?! Perhaps you have arachibutyrophobia (the fear of getting peanut butter stuck to the roof of your mouth)? Or maybe you're allergic to peanuts? In which case, we're very sorry, but also, what are you doing with this book?

YES

You are not alone. Peanut butter is one of the world's favourite spreads, and it's not surprising when you consider that it's both delicious and full of good things: unsaturated fats (the healthy ones), fibre, protein, potassium, antioxidants, vitamins (B and E) and minerals (magnesium, iron and zinc).

The Incas and Aztecs in the Americas might have been the first people to discover the joys of peanuts smashed into paste, and people in Africa and China have been grinding peanuts into stews and sauces for centuries. In the US, peanut butter could be considered a culinary treasure: Americans eat enough of the delicious stuff every year to coat the floor of the Grand Canyon. They even have a national day to celebrate it, not to mention days for peanut butter lovers, peanut butter cookies and peanut butter fudge. Its super-high nutritional content means that peanut butter is now being used across the world to beat malnutrition. What *can't* peanut butter do?

Everyone loves PB on toast, in sandwiches, coated in chocolate or just straight out of the jar – and there's absolutely nothing wrong with that! But peanut butter truly belongs in every meal, whether that's breakfast, lunch, dinner or an all-important midnight snack. This book has recipes for old and new favourites for all times of day, although don't feel constricted: in the same way that peanut butter on toast is perfect at any hour, peanut butter granola (page 20) definitely works for dinner, peanut butter curry (page 68) makes a great midnight snack, and there's no reason why you can't have a peanut butter brownie (page 112) for breakfast every now and then.

DO YOU WANT TO MAKE PEANUT BUTTER FROM SCRATCH?

 NO

Fair enough – life can be busy and you never want to be caught without a jar of the good stuff in your pantry. Luckily, there are more and more great peanut butters available. But read your labels to make sure that you really *are* buying the good stuff.

Remember these fun facts about peanut butter's most important ingredient:

- Peanuts are not actually nuts at all – they are legumes, which means that they're related to peas, lentils and beans. Also, they grow underground! This is not going to help you when buying peanut butter, but still, fun facts!

- Hi-oleic peanuts are a special type of peanut containing more oleic acid, which is an unsaturated (or good) fat. The fat profile of hi-oleic peanuts is close to that of avocado oil (healthy!), plus the oleic acid also makes the peanuts stay tasty for longer and gives them extra crunch.

- Peanuts are grown all around the world, with China the largest producer, but it's always good to look for peanuts that are grown locally to you – that should mean a fresher product and fewer food miles.

Most delicious peanut butters will just have peanuts and salt on the ingredients list, and in some cases not even the salt (that's a personal choice thing). This means that they are vegan and gluten free.

There are some fancy peanut butters out there; don't be afraid to try ones with cinnamon, honey, pepper or other seeds included to change up your PB game. But there are certain things that peanut butter definitely shouldn't have in it. If you see any of the following on a label, run the other way.

Sugar: too many processed foods have added sugar or other sweeteners, but peanuts are already naturally sweet – no sugar required. (Xylitol, a common added sweetener in PB, can also be poisonous to dogs, so keep that front of mind before considering feeding your furry friend any PB treats, or turn to page 146 to learn how to make our special dog PB.)

Oil: again, peanuts produce their own natural oils, so there's no need to add any extra. Added oils just means added saturated (unhealthy) fats. Some brands even add palm oil, which is pretty terrible for the orangutans (ruining their fast-dwindling habitat), not just bad for you.

Numbers: some peanut butters have weird additives to artificially thicken, flavour or preserve them. This is particularly an issue with 'light' peanut butters – avoid these! If you want healthier PB, just leave out the salt.

You might need to give your 'good stuff' peanut butter a stir every now and then, as the natural oils can separate a bit without added chemicals, but that just gives you another excuse to lick the spoon.

YES!

Great idea – making your own peanut butter is pretty easy and extra yum. Turn the page to find out how.

As we already know, peanut butter usually consists of one or two things: peanuts and maybe some salt.

The real secret to delicious flavour and a silky-smooth texture (or the perfect crunch) is in dry-roasting your peanuts. So the first step to making peanut butter is to preheat your oven to 170°C (340°F).

Take some fresh, good-quality shelled peanuts and scatter them over a baking tray. If you use 2 cups of peanuts, you'll get about 1½ cups of peanut butter.

Roast the peanuts for 20–25 minutes or until golden or dark golden, depending on the flavour you like: the more roasted the peanut, the more intense the taste. Make sure you cool them for at least 5 minutes before turning them into butter (and try not to snack on too many in that time!). You're almost ready to start blending, but first, some important notes.

· ·

- Keep your home-made peanut butter in sterilised glass jars. To sterilise jars, wash them (including the lids) in a dishwasher on a slow cycle, then air-dry them on a clean tea towel (dish towel). Alternatively, preheat the oven to 120°C (250°F). Wash the jars and lids in hot, soapy water, then place them on a baking tray and transfer to the oven for 20 minutes to fully dry out.

- Peanut butter should always be stored in a dark, cool pantry. It doesn't need to be refrigerated unless you're not going to use it within a few months, but when would that ever happen?

- For all of the recipes in this book, feel free to use any type of peanut butter: bought or home-made, crunchy or smooth, salty, fancy or just straight peanutty.

NOW, THE BIG QUESTION. DO YOU LIKE YOUR PEANUT BUTTER ...

SMOOTH?

Take your dry-roasted peanuts and put them in a food processor. Turn it on and let it run for 5 minutes. The peanuts will start off by turning into a dry ball, but don't panic. Just scrape down the sides of the food processor and continue to blend until you've got a creamy, delicious smooth paste.

Then, right at the end, add the salt. We recommend 1–2 teaspoons of salt for every 2 cups of peanuts, but you might want more or less or even none – it's all about your tastebuds.

CRUNCHY?

We'll let you in on a secret: while some crunchy peanut butters are smooth peanut butters that haven't been totally blended, most crunchy peanut butters are actually *smooth* peanut butter with some crunchy bits just added back in.

So once you've dry-roasted your peanuts, take a handful and quickly pulse them in the food processor. Set them aside and go about making smooth peanut butter as usual with the remaining peanuts, then thoroughly mix the crunchy nuts back through the smooth paste using a spoon. Ta da: crunchy peanut butter! We like 1 part crunch to 5 parts smooth, but again, you do you.

FANCY?

Try experimenting by adding different flavours to your peanut butter. Mixing in some honey is an easy one, or how about some melted dark chocolate? Perhaps vanilla extract, maple syrup or chia seeds? A sprinkling of cinnamon and a handful of raisins is one of our personal favourites. There's no specific recipe: just add ingredients to taste and stir.

WOULD YOU LIKE PEANUT BUTTER FOR...

DO YOU WANT AN EASY WAY TO FIND
ALL THE RECIPES IN THIS BOOK?

WHO ARE
TIM + JAMES?

Everyone dreams about making peanut butter in paradise, don't they? We definitely did, and now we're living that dream, leading the PB revolution from Byron Bay, Australia.

We are US-born Tim Lannan and Aussie James Annabel (and Frankie the staffy). As PB enthusiasts, we wanted to make a natural peanut butter that would support local workers and farmers. We first made our peanut butter to sell at the local Byron Bay markets, but then we got an order for a whole pallet, and then another. We had to learn how to smash peanuts really fast! From humble beginnings, we now send our peanut butter all over the world, and we even have a shop in Byron selling all things PB.

We believe that peanut butter deserves a spot as an essential pantry item. After all, we use it every day, and not just on toast. This collection of delicious recipes is influenced by our travels and perfected in our kitchen at home. So pick up the spoon, turn the lid and let us take you on a PB foodie safari with our favourite nutty recipes.

And in the meantime, you'll either find us surfing or smashing peanuts here in Byron.

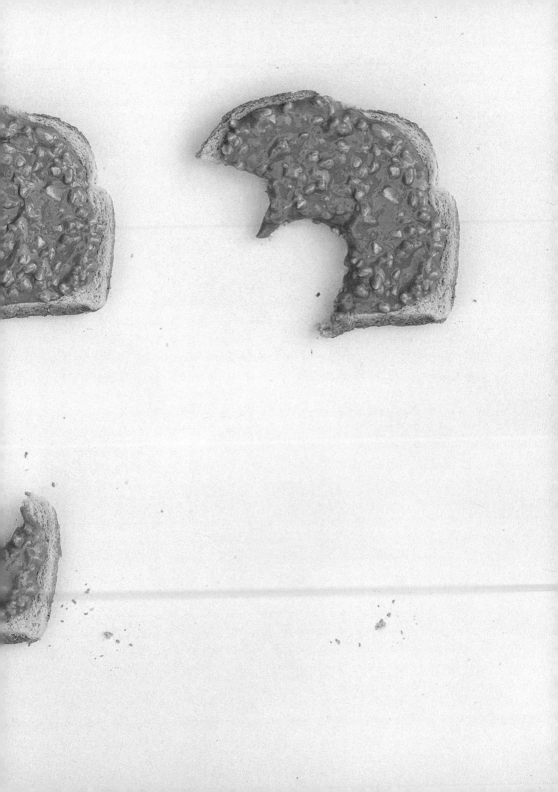

PEANUT BUTTER

FOR BREAKFAST

CRUNCHY GRANOLA

Makes 10–12 serves

60 ml (2 fl oz/¼ cup)
  coconut oil
125 ml (4 fl oz/½ cup)
  brown rice syrup
150 g (5½ oz/2¾ cups)
  coconut chips
200 g (7 oz) peanut butter
125 g (4½ oz/1 cup)
  sunflower kernels
200 g (7 oz/2 cups)
  rolled (porridge) oats
½ teaspoon Himalayan salt

➜ FOR CHOCOLATE

100 g (3½ oz) chocolate
  chips or cacao nibs

➜ FOR MIXED FRUIT

125 g (4½ oz/1 cup) raisins
100 g (3½ oz) cranberries

Obviously peanut butter has always been comfortable on the breakfast table, but it really works in this moreish granola. You've got two options: keep things nice with mixed fruit, or make it naughty with chocolate chips. Serve granola with your favourite milk or yoghurt and topped with fresh fruit, scatter some over your smoothies or smoothie bowls, or just eat it by the handful.

. . . .

Preheat the oven to 180°C (350°F) and line a baking tray with baking paper.

Heat the coconut oil and rice syrup in a small saucepan over a low heat until just melted but not boiling. Stir thoroughly and remove from the heat.

Combine the coconut chips, peanut butter, sunflower kernels, oats and salt in a large bowl. If making mixed fruit granola, add the raisins and cranberries. Mix thoroughly. Add the melted coconut oil and rice syrup to the bowl and stir until evenly combined.

Spread in a thin, even layer on the prepared tray. Bake for approximately 8 minutes, until golden brown, then cool completely on the tray. If making the chocolate granola, mix in the chocolate chips.

Store in an airtight container in a cool place for up to 6 weeks.

EASY-AS NO-BAKE GRANOLA BARS

Makes 12 pieces

250 ml (8½ fl oz/1 cup) brown
   rice syrup
125 g (4 oz/½ cup) smooth
   peanut butter
3 tablespoons coconut oil
2 teaspoons natural
   vanilla extract
200 g (7 oz/2 cups)
   rolled (porridge) oats
¼ teaspoon salt
100 g (3½ oz/⅔ cup) mixed
   dried fruit
80 g (2¾ oz/½ cup) mixed
   nuts and/or seeds
80 g (2¾ oz/½ cup) chocolate
   chips and/or cacao nibs

As breakfast aficionados, we'd always recommend sitting down to enjoy arguably the day's best meal, but some mornings there just isn't time. If you need breakfast on the run, these quick and easy granola bars can be prepared the night before, no cooking required. They make a great lunchbox or hiking snack as well.

. . . .

Line a medium 18 × 28 cm (7 × 11 in) baking tray with aluminium foil or baking paper. Generously grease the foil or paper.

Combine the rice syrup, peanut butter and coconut oil in a small saucepan over a medium–low heat and warm gently until melted and smooth, stirring frequently. Remove from the heat and stir through the vanilla extract. Set aside to cool for 5–10 minutes.

In a large mixing bowl, combine the oats, salt, dried fruit, nuts/seeds and chocolate chips, and mix well. Add the peanut butter mixture and stir until mixed evenly. Scoop into the prepared tin, then press into an even layer using clean fingers, a spatula or the back of a spoon.

Refrigerate for at least 2 hours or overnight. Slice into bars using a very sharp knife. Store in an airtight container in the refrigerator for up to 3 weeks.

PIMP MY OVERNIGHT OATS

Serves 3–4

100 g (3½ oz/1 cup) rolled
  (porridge) oats
375 ml (12½ fl oz/1½ cups) milk
  of your choice
3 tablespoons peanut butter
240 g (8½ oz/1 cup) mashed
  ripe banana, plus extra,
  sliced, to serve (optional)
75 g (2¾ oz/⅓ cup) mixed
  berries or other sliced fruit,
  plus extra to serve
75 g (2¾ oz/½ cup) dried fruit,
  plus extra to serve

Another easy, make-and-refrigerate recipe to
prepare the night before if you need to dash out
the door the next morning, or if you want an energy
boost after the gym. Go crazy adding any of your
favourite berries or other garnishes.

. . . .

Pour the oats into a large bowl. Pour in the milk,
add the peanut butter and stir well.

Add the banana, berries and dried fruit and stir until
well combined.

Spoon into cups or serving bowls, then cover
and refrigerate for at least 6 hours or up to 3 days.

Top with extra banana, berries or dried fruit
to serve.

PB+J BREAKFAST PARFAIT

Serves 3

550 g (1 lb 3 oz) yoghurt
  of your choice
3 tablespoons peanut butter
3 tablespoons Quick and
  easy berry chia jam (below)
  or other berry jam
Crunchy granola (page 20) and
  sliced strawberries, to serve

Quick and easy berry chia jam
750 g (1 lb 11 oz/5 cups) frozen
  mixed berries or fruit of
  your choice
45 g (1½ oz/¼ cup) chia seeds
2 tablespoons orange juice
  (from ½ orange)
60 ml (2 fl oz/¼ cup) maple
  syrup or sweetener of choice
  (optional)

It's hard to pick the best PB combo, but PB+J must be pretty far up the list. Layer the flavour with yoghurt, PB and a Quick and easy berry chia jam (or jelly, for our American friends). If you're scared of making jam, don't be put off by this one! It really is so simple, and you'll love it on your toast, pancakes, waffles and bagels as well.

. . . .

To make the chia jam, combine the berries, chia seeds and orange juice in a medium bowl and stir well. Cover and set aside at room temperature for 1–2 hours, or refrigerate overnight, to thaw.

Use a potato masher, fork or spatula to mash to your desired consistency. Add syrup to taste. Set aside for 20–30 minutes, for the chia seeds to absorb the moisture and expand.

For each parfait, divide about half the yoghurt between serving jars or bowls. Top with layers of peanut butter and jam. Repeat each layer and refrigerate until ready to serve, up to 3 days.

Top with granola and strawberries to serve.

SMOOTHIE BOWLS

Each serves 2

We have absolutely nothing against smoothies (see page 123 for proof) but sometimes you really just want to eat something with a spoon. Tropical acai and dragon fruit both make for smoothie bowls that are super healthy and look like a work of art. Amplify the nutritional value with your favourite protein powders or supplements, or decorate with fresh fruit and edible flowers for a totally beautiful breakfast. And note, it will make your life (and your blender's) much easier if you cut the bananas up before freezing them.

· ·

Place all ingredients for your chosen bowl in a high-speed blender. Blend slowly, starting low then increasing the speed, until completely smooth.

Pour into bowls and top with your choice of garnishes.

⟶ Pictured overleaf

EVERY GOOD SMOOTHIE BOWL STARTS HERE

250 ml (8½ fl oz/1 cup) coconut milk or milk of your choice

2 frozen bananas · 2 tablespoons peanut butter

300 g (10½ oz/2 cups) fresh or frozen berries

PICK A FLAVOUR

ACAI

100 g (3½ oz) frozen acai berry or
4 teaspoons acai berry powder

1–2 tablespoons honey or maple syrup
(optional)

DRAGON FRUIT

100 g (3½ oz) frozen dragon fruit

3 tablespoons vanilla protein powder

THEN CHOOSE YOUR TOPPINGS

coconut flakes · fresh or dried fruit · edible flowers

cacao nibs · peanut butter · Crunchy granola (page 20)

BEST BANANA BREAD

Makes 8–10 slices

3 overripe bananas, mashed,
plus extra, sliced lengthways,
to top
125 g (4½ oz/½ cup)
peanut butter
125 ml (4 fl oz/½ cup) coconut oil
125 ml (4 fl oz/½ cup) coconut,
rice or maple syrup
80 g (2¾ oz/½ cup) chopped
dates, soaked in warm water
for 10 minutes then drained
2 eggs or egg substitute
1 teaspoon natural vanilla extract
280 g (10 oz/2¾ cups) almond
meal
40 g (1½ oz/¼ cup) coconut sugar
30 g (1 oz/½ cup) shredded
coconut
2 teaspoons ground cinnamon
1½ teaspoons baking powder
1½ teaspoons bicarbonate of
soda (baking soda)

We love that everyone calls it 'banana bread' to pretend that we're not just eating cake for breakfast, but this recipe is so full of good things that you don't even need to feel guilty about it. Serve it warm, cold or toasted, either on its own or with extra mashed banana and peanut butter (of course).

. . . .

Preheat the oven to 180°C (350°F) and grease a 23 × 13 cm (9 × 5 in) loaf (bar) tin.

Combine the banana, peanut butter, coconut oil, syrup, dates, egg and vanilla in a large bowl and mix well. Add the remaining ingredients along with a pinch of salt, and stir until just combined, taking care not to overmix. Pour into the prepared tin and top with the extra banana.

Bake for 25 minutes or until golden brown and a skewer inserted in the centre comes out clean. Cool in the tin for 10 minutes, then transfer to a wire rack to cool completely. Store in an airtight container in the refrigerator for 4–5 days.

LOADED TOAST

Make the most of your toast! Get a slice of your favourite sourdough or seedy loaf, or switch things up with a bagel or crumpet. Pop it in the toaster, spread on your PB and get creative with toppings. Aside from good old PB+J (perhaps using the jam from page 27), we've got a few more ideas here to get you started. The possibilities are endless, and when peanut butter is involved, the results are guaranteed to be delicious.

SAVOURY BITES

Smashed avocado, hot sauce and a sprinkle of sesame seeds

Caramelised banana, bacon (or coconut bacon) and maple syrup

Hot sauce and sliced pickles (really!)

SWEET SENSATIONS

Berry yoghurt and fresh berries

Dried or fresh fruit with cacao nibs or chocolate shavings

Baked apple and Coconut salted caramel (pages 108–9)

Toasted marshmallows on chocolate PB (for the kids, or big kids)

NOT-SO-BASIC BERRY MUFFINS

Makes 8

335 g (12 oz/2¼ cups)
   self-raising flour
2 teaspoons ground cinnamon
40 g (1½ oz/¼ cup)
   coconut sugar
250 g (9 oz/1⅔ cups)
   frozen berries
   (we used raspberries
   and blueberries)
80 g (2¾ oz) unsalted butter
   or butter substitute,
   melted and cooled
250 ml (8½ fl oz/1 cup)
   coconut, rice or maple syrup
125 g (4½ oz/½ cup)
   peanut butter, plus
   extra to serve
250 ml (8½ fl oz/1 cup)
   milk of your choice
2 eggs, lightly whisked,
   or egg substitute
1 teaspoon natural
   vanilla extract
crushed peanuts, to garnish

Before we suggest another version of cake-for-breakfast, let's recap the health benefits of peanut butter. PB contains potassium and protein, which lower the risk of high blood pressure, stroke and heart disease. It's high in fibre, so it's good for bowel health, and has magnesium to fortify your bones and muscles. Plus there are all those healthy fats, vitamins and antioxidants. Now, go eat a breakfast muffin – it's got fruit in it too!

· · · · · · · · · · · · · · · · · · · ·

Preheat the oven to 180°C (350°F). Grease eight holes of a 12-hole standard muffin tin or line with baking paper or cases.

Sift the flour and cinnamon into a large bowl and stir through the coconut sugar, berries and a pinch of salt. In another large bowl, combine the butter, syrup, peanut butter, milk, egg and vanilla, and mix thoroughly. Gently fold the syrup mixture into the flour mixture until just combined, taking care not to overmix. Spoon into the prepared muffin tin.

Bake for 20–25 minutes or until golden brown and a skewer inserted in the centre of a muffin comes out clean. Cool in the tin for 10 minutes, then transfer to a wire rack to cool completely.

Serve dolloped with an extra spoonful of peanut butter and a sprinkle of crushed peanuts. Store in an airtight container for 4–5 days.

DREAMY CHOC-CHIP PANCAKES

Serves 2–3

185 g (6½ oz/1¼ cups) plain
   (all-purpose) flour
1 tablespoon baking powder
3 tablespoons sugar
¼ teaspoon salt
250 ml (8½ fl oz/1 cup) milk
   of your choice
1 egg, lightly beaten, or egg
   substitute
60 g (2 oz/¼ cup) peanut
   butter, softened, plus extra
   to serve
100 g (3½ oz) chocolate chips
   or cacao nibs, plus extra
   to serve
oil of your choice, for frying

Breakfast food doesn't get much better than pancakes. But it can! Add chocolate chips and peanut butter, and you've got something that's worth serving up at any time of day.

. . . .

Sift the flour and baking powder into a large bowl, then stir in the sugar and salt. Add the milk and egg and whisk gently to combine. Stir in the peanut butter and fold through the chocolate chips.

Warm a little oil in a small frying pan over a medium heat and pour in 60 ml (2 fl oz/¼ cup) of batter. Cook until small bubbles appear on the surface and the edges start to look dry, then flip and cook the other side for about 3 minutes, until both sides are golden brown.

Layer your stack with extra peanut butter, top with chocolate chips and serve immediately.

⟶ Pictured page 42

SYRUPY WAFFLES

Serves 2–3

300 g (10½ oz/2 cups)
   plain (all-purpose) flour
1 tablespoon baking powder
55 g (2 oz/¼ cup) caster
   (superfine) sugar
¼ teaspoon salt
2 eggs or egg substitute
500 ml (17 fl oz/2 cups)
   milk of your choice
60 ml (2 fl oz/¼ cup)
   coconut oil
1 teaspoon natural vanilla
   extract
125 g (4½ oz/½ cup)
   peanut butter

Peanut butter syrup
145 g (5 oz/⅔ cup) caster
   (superfine) sugar
90 g (3 oz/⅓ cup) peanut butter
½ teaspoon natural
   vanilla extract

Optional toppings
fresh fruit, Banana nice cream
   (page 107), Quick and easy
   berry chia jam (page 27)

These are so good. In fact, they're probably one of our favourite treats in the book, which is saying something. If you've got a waffle maker, then look no further for your next slow-Sunday-morning brunch. You could switch up the peanut butter syrup with Coconut salted caramel (pages 108–9) or Salted dark chocolate sauce (pages 112–13).

. . . .

To make the syrup, combine the sugar and 125 ml (4 fl oz/½ cup) water in a small saucepan and bring to a full rolling boil. Immediately remove from the heat and stir in the peanut butter and vanilla. Continue stirring until the peanut butter is melted and the syrup is smooth. Set aside to cool and thicken.

Preheat a non-stick waffle iron.

Sift the flour and baking powder into a large bowl and stir through the sugar and salt. In another large bowl, whisk together the eggs, milk, oil, vanilla and peanut butter until smooth. Gently fold the dry ingredients into the egg mixture until just combined.

Cook in the waffle iron and serve warm in a stack, layered with the peanut butter syrup and your choice of other toppings.

⟶ Pictured page 43

PEANUT BUTTER

FOR LUNCH

SATAY SKEWERS WITH ALL THE SAUCES

Makes 6–8 skewers and
approximately 300 g
(10 ½ oz) sauce

Skewers

500 g (1 lb 2 oz) protein food
  (e.g. firm tofu, haloumi,
  meat), cut into 2.5 cm
  (1 in) cubes
270 g (9½ oz) quick-cooking
  vegetables
  (e.g. eggplant/aubergine,
  mushrooms, zucchini/
  courgette, capsicum/bell
  pepper, jack fruit, cherry
  tomatoes, baby corn), cut
  into 2.5 cm (1 in) wedges
6–8 bamboo skewers, soaked
  in water for 30 minutes
coriander (cilantro) leaves,
  to garnish
steamed brown rice and
  choice of green vegetables,
  to serve

No barbecue lunch is complete without skewers, and they're almost as fun to make as they are to eat. We've given you three takes on our ultimate satay sauce: original, red curry and smoky barbecue. Make sure you've got plenty for both marinating and dipping. There's no shortage of ways to use up any leftover sauce, but perhaps start with Jackfruit curry satay (page 78) or Smoky barbecue tacos (page 61).

. . . .

To make the satay sauce, heat the oil in a small saucepan over a medium heat. Add the garlic, onion powder, lemongrass and chilli, along with the curry powder if making the red curry satay. Fry until aromatic. Add the remaining ingredients for your chosen sauce to the pan. Bring to a simmer for 5–8 minutes, until the sauce turns smooth. Remove from the heat.

Thread your chosen protein food and chopped vegetables on the skewers and coat in the satay sauce, leaving enough sauce for dipping. Either marinate in an airtight container in the refrigerator overnight or cook immediately.

Preheat the barbecue to medium–high. Grill the skewers for 4–5 minutes, until lightly charred.

Garnish with coriander and serve with the rice, green vegetables and remaining satay sauce on the side.

⟶ Pictured overleaf

START HERE FOR AN AMAZING SATAY SAUCE

1 tablespoon coconut oil · 2 garlic cloves, finely chopped

½ teaspoon onion powder · 1 teaspoon finely chopped lemongrass (white part only)

½ teaspoon finely chopped chilli · 250 g (9 oz/1 cup) peanut butter

80 ml (2½ fl oz/⅓ cup) water · 1 tablespoon lime juice

THEN CHOOSE YOUR FLAVOUR

ORIGINAL

80 ml (2½ fl oz/⅓ cup) coconut milk

1–2 tablespoons raw (demerara) sugar

1 teaspoon tamarind pulp

RED CURRY

1 tablespoon red curry powder

80 ml (2½ fl oz/⅓ cup) coconut milk

90 g (3 oz/⅓ cup) tomato paste
(concentrated purée)

SMOKY BARBECUE

60 ml (2 fl oz/¼ cup) coconut milk · 60 ml (2 fl oz/¼ cup) tomato sauce (ketchup)

2 tablespoons molasses · 1 teaspoon raw (demerara) sugar

60 g (2 oz/¼ cup) tomato paste (concentrated purée) · 1 teaspoon tamarind pulp

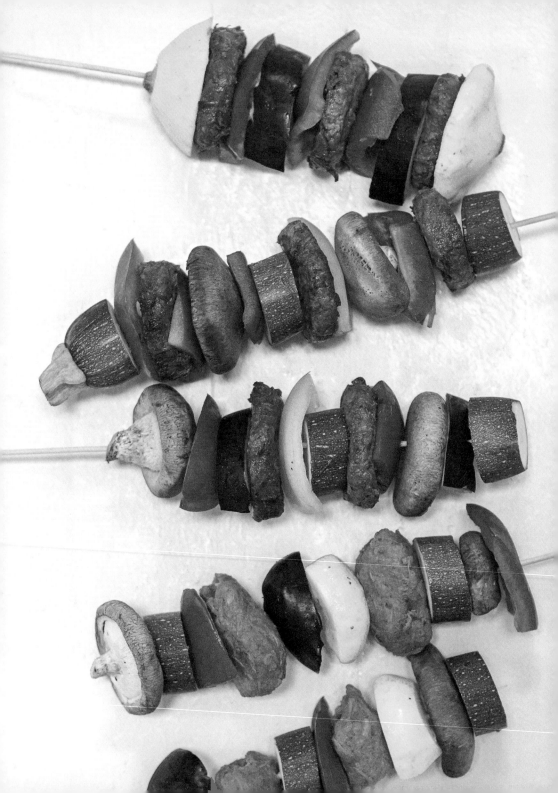

BUTTERY BALSAMIC BRUSCHETTA

Makes 4–6 pieces

250 ml (8½ fl oz/1 cup)
   balsamic vinegar
3 tablespoons olive oil
2 large tomatoes, seeds
   removed, diced
4–6 large strawberries, diced
1 handful fresh basil leaves,
   chopped
1 baguette or rustic
   bread loaf
3 tablespoons peanut butter

This bruschetta is almost like a savoury take on PB+J!
Strawberries make it extra summery.

. . . .

Make a balsamic reduction by pouring the balsamic
vinegar into a small saucepan over a medium
heat. Bring to the boil, then reduce the heat to
medium–low and simmer for 10–15 minutes until
thick enough to coat the back of a spoon. Remove
from the heat and set aside to cool. The reduction
will thicken more as it cools. Once cool, store in a
glass jar with an airtight lid in the refrigerator for
up to 3 months.

Preheat the oven to 180°C (350°F).

In a medium bowl combine 2 tablespoons of the olive
oil with the tomato, strawberry and basil. Toss to
coat, then refrigerate for 20–30 minutes to bring out
the flavours.

Cut the bread into thin slices, then lightly brush one
side of each slice with the remaining oil. Lay the
bread, oiled side up, on a baking tray and bake for
8–10 minutes, until the tops are golden brown.

Allow the bread to cool for a couple of minutes, then
spread with the peanut butter. Top with the tomato
mixture, then drizzle with the balsamic reduction.

RAINBOW ROLLS

Makes 8

8 spring-roll wrappers
1 beetroot (beet), grated
155 g (5½ oz/1 cup) mixed
    chopped yellow and red
    capsicum (bell pepper)
150 g (5½ oz/1 cup) thinly sliced
    carrot
200 g (7 oz) firm tofu, thinly
    sliced
1 mango, thinly sliced
1 handful coriander (cilantro)
    leaves
1 handful mint leaves

**Ginger peanut butter
dipping sauce**
125 g (4½ oz/½ cup) peanut
    butter
1½ tablespoons soy sauce
    or tamari
juice of ½ lime
2 tablespoons soft brown sugar
    or maple syrup
½ teaspoon grated fresh ginger

Get everyone involved in filling these fresh
rice-paper rolls with whatever veggies they like,
the more colour the better! Make sure there's a
little bit of each vegetable and a little (lot) of the
ginger PB dipping sauce across each roll, so that
every bite is totally satisfying.

. . . .

To make the peanut dipping sauce, combine all
the ingredients except the water in a medium
bowl and whisk together. Whisk in some hot water,
1 tablespoon at a time, until the sauce is pourable
but still thick. Set aside.

Pour hot water into a large shallow dish or frying
pan and submerge a spring-roll wrapper for
10–20 seconds until soft. Transfer to a clean, slightly
damp tea towel (dish towel) and smooth gently
until flat. Place an eighth of the beetroot, capsicum,
carrot, tofu, mango, coriander and mint in the centre
of the wrapper. Fold in the two sides, then roll up
from the bottom, holding the tension on the wrapper
until the roll is completely sealed. Cover with plastic
wrap or a damp tea towel (dish towel), then repeat
with the remaining wrappers and fillings.

Serve with the dipping sauce on the side.

RED CURRY SUSHI

Makes 6 rolls

440 g (15½ oz/2 cups) brown
   sushi rice
1 teaspoon sugar
½ teaspoon salt
2 teaspoons vinegar
2 avocados
1 carrot
1 cucumber
6 nori sheets
Red curry satay sauce
   (pages 46–7)
pickled ginger, to serve
crushed peanuts, to garnish

Can't lie, we do love a fusion, especially when it's
fusing a few of our favourite things: Japanese sushi
rolls, a kick of Thai red curry and, of course, peanut
butter. You'll find sushi mats in most international
sections of grocery stores.

. . . .

Cook the sushi rice according to the packet
directions. In a small bowl, stir together the sugar,
salt and vinegar. Mix the cooked rice with the
sugar mixture, then cover and set aside to cool to
room temperature for 15 minutes (transfer to the
refrigerator if you're not ready by then).

Cut the avocados, carrot and cucumber into thin
strips. Wrap your sushi mat in plastic wrap to prevent
rice sticking to it. Lay the mat on a clean work
surface with the bamboo slats running crossways.
Lay a nori sheet, rough side up, on the sushi mat.
Using a wet spatula and taking care not tear the nori,
cover with a thin layer of rice, leaving about 2 cm
(¾ in) bare at the top and bottom. Lay the fillings
across the centre of the sheet and drizzle with red
curry satay sauce. Roll into a firm log shape from the
bottom up, using the sushi mat to keep tension on
the roll as you go.

Dip a very sharp knife in water, shake off any excess
water and cut the roll into slices using long strokes.
Serve with pickled ginger and extra red curry satay
sauce garnished with crushed peanuts for dipping.

MEZZE PLATE

Serves 2–3

Peanut butter hummus

400 g (14 oz) tinned chickpeas
60 g (2 oz/¼ cup) peanut butter
2 tablespoons peanut or
  olive oil
1 garlic clove, crushed
¼ teaspoon lemon juice
¼ teaspoon salt

Peanut butter falafel

440 g (15½ oz/2 cups) dried
  chickpeas
1 teaspoon cumin seeds
1 teaspoon coriander seeds
60 g (2 oz/¼ cup) crunchy
  peanut butter
1 onion, chopped
3 garlic cloves, finely chopped
zest of 1 lemon
2 tablespoons finely chopped
  flat-leaf (Italian) parsley
2 tablespoons finely chopped
  fresh coriander (cilantro)
2 teaspoons salt
½ teaspoon ground black
  pepper

It is a truth universally acknowledged that everyone loves hummus and falafel. It is obviously also true that everyone loves peanut butter, which seems like a pretty good reason to combine them all into the spread of your dreams. This mezze looks pretty and tastes pretty darn good, whether laid out on a grazing table or packed up in a lunchbox or picnic basket. You'll need to soak the chickpeas ahead of time to make the falafel.

· ·

To make the hummus, drain and rinse the chickpeas, then blend all the ingredients with 80 ml (2½ fl oz/⅓ cup) water in a food processor until smooth. Transfer to a serving bowl, then cover and refrigerate until ready to serve.

To make the falafel, put the chickpeas in a large bowl and cover with water to at least 5 cm (2 in) above the chickpeas. Set aside to soak for at least 8 hours or overnight, then drain and rinse.

Heat the cumin and coriander seeds in a dry frying pan over a low heat until aromatic and beginning to brown. Transfer to a mortar or spice grinder and grind as finely as possible.

Transfer the drained chickpeas to a food processor and add the spices, peanut butter, onion, garlic, lemon zest, herbs, salt and pepper. Pulse until blended, taking care not to over-blend. Sprinkle in

3 tablespoons flour of your
  choice, plus extra as needed
1 teaspoon baking powder
peanut or grape seed oil,
  for frying

Options to serve
pide (Turkish flat bread)
carrots
roasted and fresh capsicum
  (bell pepper)
broccoli florets
gherkins (pickles)
pickled onions
tahini, for drizzling

the flour and baking powder, and pulse until the mixture has a dough-like texture. Transfer to a large bowl, then cover and refrigerate for 2 hours.

Using clean, damp hands, form 1–2 tablespoon portions of the chickpea mixture into balls. If they don't hold together, mix in a little more flour.

Fill a large pan or wok with peanut oil to a depth of 7.5 cm (3 in) and place over a medium–high heat until the oil begins to shimmer. Working in batches, fry the falafel until golden brown on both sides, taking care not to overcrowd the pan and turning after 2–3 minutes. Keep warm in a low oven on a baking tray lined with paper towel while you cook the remaining falafel.

Arrange the serving ingredients on a platter and serve with the hummus and falafel.

⟶ Pictured overleaf

SMOKY BARBECUE TACOS

Makes 6–8 tacos

2 tablespoons peanut oil or
  your oil of choice
450 g (1 lb) protein food
  (e.g. beef, cooked beans,
  tofu, seitan)
80 g (2¾ oz/½ cup) finely
  chopped red onion, plus extra
  to serve
1 teaspoon Mexican-style
  chilli powder
½ teaspoon ground cumin
1 large avocado
juice of 1 lime
12–16 corn or flour tortillas
270 g (9½ oz/6 cups, loosely
  packed) baby spinach or
  mixed greens
2 tablespoons roughly chopped
  coriander (cilantro) leaves
Smoky barbecue satay sauce
  (pages 46–7)
grated cheese, sour cream
  or plain yoghurt (optional)
sliced fresh chilli, to serve
  (optional)

Tim, being an American, of course loves barbecue, so we had to make something a bit Tex-Mex with peanut butter. This is a flavour explosion, with the sweet molasses in the Smoky barbecue satay sauce playing against the spicy Mexican chilli powder.

· ·

Heat the oil in a large frying pan over a medium heat and sauté your chosen protein food. Add the onion, chilli powder and cumin and cook for about 5 minutes, until the onions are soft, adding a little water if necessary to keep the mixture moist.

Meanwhile, slice the avocado and sprinkle with the lime juice to prevent browning.

To serve, layer up two tortillas together and add some greens, then spoon over the protein mixture. Top with the avocado, coriander, extra red onion, smoky barbecue satay sauce and any other toppings of your choosing, and finish with some sliced chilli if you're feeling brave.

THAI GINGER SALAD

Serves 2–3 as a main,
4–6 as a side

300 g (10½ oz/4 cups)
  shredded cabbage
155 g (5½ oz/1 cup grated
  carrot
1 cucumber, halved
  lengthways, seeds removed
  and thinly sliced
60 g (2 oz/1 cup) cooked
  shelled edamame
2 onions, thinly sliced
1 handful coriander (cilantro)
  leaves, plus extra, to garnish
chopped peanuts, to garnish

Peanut butter dressing
60 g (2 oz/¼ cup) crunchy
  peanut butter
2 tablespoons rice vinegar
3 tablespoons toasted
  sesame oil
2 tablespoons lime juice
1 tablespoon soy sauce or
  tamari
pinch of thinly sliced
  fresh ginger
1 teaspoon salt

Peanuts have become core to many South-East Asian cuisines, including Malaysian and Thai food. If you love crunch, this Thai-inspired salad is for you. Serve it as a side for your Satay skewers (pages 46–7) or just tuck in for a simple and delicious summer lunch.

To make the dressing, whiz all the ingredients together in a food processor or blender.

Combine all the coleslaw ingredients, except the garnishes, in a salad bowl, pour over the dressing and mix well. Garnish with the chopped peanuts and extra coriander to serve.

GREEN APPLE SALAD

Serves 2 as a main,
3–4 as a side

4 largish green apples
1 tablespoon lemon juice
2 tablespoons raisins or
    sultanas
200 g (7 oz/4 cups) English
    spinach leaves or salad
    greens of your choice
chopped peanuts, to garnish

Apple cider vinegar dressing

1 tablespoon apple cider
    vinegar
1 tablespoon olive oil
2 teaspoons smooth
    peanut butter

Another fresh and crunchy salad that makes a great addition to your barbecue lunch spread. Apples and peanut butter are a classic snack combo; this just fancies things up a bit.

To make the dressing, whiz all the ingredients together in a food processor or blender.

Using a mandoline or sharp knife, thinly slice the apples. Mix with the lemon juice and raisins and set aside.

Line serving bowls with the spinach and top with the apple mixture. Pour over the dressing and garnish with the chopped peanuts.

PEANUT BUTTER

FOR DINNER

COCONUT CURRY

Serves 2–3

400 ml (13½ fl oz) tinned
 coconut milk
125 g (4½ oz/½ cup) smooth
 peanut butter
1 garlic clove, finely chopped
2 red chillies, finely chopped
2 teaspoons curry powder
2 tablespoons grated fresh
 ginger
200 g (7 oz/1 cup) chopped
 tomatoes
2 tablespoons coconut oil
 or oil of your choice
400 g (14 oz) protein food
 (e.g. firm tofu)
125 g (4½ oz/¼ cup) sliced
 green beans
400 g (14 oz) cooked
 pumpkin (winter squash)
 or sweet potato, cubed
steamed brown rice, to serve
chopped coriander (cilantro),
 chilli and peanuts, to
 garnish

Peanuts appear in curries throughout Asia. This dish takes inspiration from both Thai and Indian food, combining PB with creamy coconut milk and curry powder. You might want to adjust the chilli, depending on how you spicy you like things.

. . . .

Blend the coconut milk, peanut butter, garlic, chillies, curry powder, ginger and tomatoes to a paste in a food processor.

Heat the oil in a medium saucepan over a medium heat and cook your chosen protein food. Transfer the protein to a plate and return the saucepan to a medium heat. Add the peanut butter curry paste and cook, stirring frequently, for 5 minutes. Reduce the heat to medium–low and simmer, covered, for another 5 minutes. Return the protein food to the pan and add the green beans and pumpkin or sweet potato, then cover and simmer for another 10 minutes or until the beans are cooked.

Serve the curry on the rice, garnished with the coriander, chilli and peanuts.

STICKY GINGER STIR-FRY

Serves 3–4

60 ml (2 fl oz/¼ cup) sesame oil
400 g (14 oz) protein food
 (e.g. firm tofu)
90 g (3 oz/¼ cup) honey or
 coconut syrup
1 large red capsicum (bell
 pepper), thinly sliced
1 large green capsicum
 (bell pepper), thinly sliced
80 g (2¾ oz/½ cup) thinly
 sliced carrot
1 chilli, thinly sliced
3 garlic cloves, finely chopped
1 teaspoon finely chopped ginger
3 tablespoons soy sauce or
 tamari
2 tablespoons rice vinegar
3 tablespoons smooth
 peanut butter
1 tablespoon cornflour
 (cornstarch)
steamed brown rice, to serve
sesame seeds, to garnish

This Chinese-inspired stir-fry is the weeknight go-to dinner that your organised self has always aspired to (you know, the self who never forgets to buy washing powder). For variety, change up the protein or add whatever veggies you've got in the refrigerator.

. . . .

Heat half the sesame oil in a large frying pan over a medium heat and cook your chosen protein food. Transfer to a plate and return the pan to the heat. Add the remaining sesame oil, honey, capsicums, carrot and chilli and cook for 4–5 minutes. Add the garlic and ginger and cook for a further 2 minutes. Return the protein food to the pan, slowly add the soy sauce, rice vinegar and peanut butter, then bring to the boil. Reduce the heat to medium–low and simmer for 3–4 minutes.

Mix the cornflour with 60 ml (2 fl oz/¼ cup) water in a small bowl until thick and smooth. Slowly add the cornflour mixture to the pan, and continue cooking until the sauce thickens.

Serve the stir-fry with the rice and garnished with sesame seeds.

PAD THAI

Serves 4–6

3 tablespoons sesame oil
2 tablespoons finely chopped
 garlic
1 large red capsicum
 (bell pepper), thinly sliced
½ red onion, chopped
250 g (9 oz) protein food
 (e.g. firm tofu), thinly sliced
50 g (1¾ oz) snow peas
 (mangetout)
120 g (4½ oz/2 cups) small
 broccoli florets
400 g (14 oz) rice-stick noodles
lime wedges, bean sprouts,
 chopped peanuts and sliced
 chilli, to garnish

Peanut sauce
110 g (4 oz/½ cup) tinned
 chickpeas
60 g (2 oz/¼ cup) peanut butter
3 tablespoons lime juice
1 tablespoon soy sauce or tamari
2 teaspoons hot sauce
125 ml (4 fl oz/½ cup) vegetable
 stock, plus extra as needed
1 teaspoon tamarind paste

Even though it's hard to play favourites when it comes to Thai food, pad Thai deserves its popularity. It's certainly James's favourite – he'll pick it every time he eats at a Thai restaurant. This recipe has the perfect balance of all those fantastic Thai flavours: salty (from the soy sauce or tamari), sour (from the tamarind and lime) and sweet (from the PB)!

. . . .

To make the Peanut sauce, drain and rinse the chickpeas, then whiz all the ingredients in a blender or food processor until smooth. Set aside.

To make the pad Thai, heat the oil in a large frying pan or wok over a medium–high heat and sauté the garlic, capsicum, onion and your chosen protein food for 5 minutes. Add the snow peas and broccoli and sauté until cooked.

Cook the rice noodles according to the packet directions. Add the drained noodles to the pan and toss. Pour in the peanut sauce and mix well. If the sauce is still too thick, slowly add enough extra stock to thin.

Serve garnished with a squeeze of lime juice, bean sprouts, peanuts and chilli.

GADO-GADO SAVOURY PIES

Serves 4

200 g (7 oz/2 sheets) frozen
    shortcrust (pie) pastry, thawed
335 g (12 oz/2 sheets) frozen
    puff pastry, thawed
1 egg, lightly beaten, or
    1–2 tablespoons olive oil,
    to glaze (optional)

Gado-gado filling
1 tablespoon olive or peanut oil
1 onion, diced
2 garlic cloves, finely chopped
1 tablespoon grated fresh ginger
1 lemongrass stem,
    white part only
1–2 kaffir lime leaves
1 teaspoon ground cumin
1 large red chilli, finely chopped
60 g (2 oz/¼ cup) crunchy
    peanut butter
1 tablespoon tamarind paste
2 tablespoons soy sauce
½ tablespoon honey or coconut
    nectar
150 g (5½ oz) firm tofu or
    tempeh, sliced and fried

Gado-gado translates as 'mix-mix' in Indonesian: tofu, potato and other vegetables are mixed together and covered with a rich peanut sauce to create one of the country's national dishes. Here we've combined those delicious elements and then wrapped them up in crispy pastry. It's a flavoursome feast that you can eat with your hands! Adjust the amount of chilli in the filling depending on how spicy you like things.

. . . .

To make the Gado-gado filling, heat the oil in a medium frying pan over a medium heat and sauté the onion for 2–3 minutes until soft. Add the garlic, ginger, lemongrass and kaffir lime leaves and sauté for another 2 minutes. Remove from the heat and stir in the cumin and chilli, then set aside for 2 minutes.

Return to the heat and add the peanut butter, tamarind paste and 500 ml (17 fl oz/2 cups) water. Bring to the boil, then reduce the heat to low and simmer for about 20 minutes, stirring occasionally, until the liquid has reduced but the mixture is still moist. Stir in the soy sauce, honey, tofu and vegetables. Remove from the heat and set aside.

Preheat oven to 220°C (430°F) and place a baking tray on the middle shelf. Grease four round 10 × 3 cm (4 × 1¼ in) pie dishes.

1 potato, diced and boiled
100 g (3½ oz) steamed green
  beans, cut into quarters
3 carrots, diced and steamed

Cut four discs of about 15 cm (6 in) diameter from both the shortcrust pastry and the puff pastry. Line the bases and sides of the prepared pie dishes with the shortcrust pastry discs. Fill with the Gado-gado, then top with the puff pastry discs, pinching the edges with the shortcrust pastry to seal and decorate. Trim off any overhanging pastry and use a pastry brush to glaze the tops with egg or oil, if using. Sit the pie dishes on the baking tray and bake for 20–25 minutes, until golden brown.

Store leftover pies in the refrigerator for 3–4 days, or freeze uncooked pies for up to 2 months before baking.

⟶ Pictured overleaf

JACKFRUIT CURRY SATAY

Serves 2–4

2 tablespoons coconut oil
1 onion, chopped
3 garlic cloves, finely
   chopped
1 teaspoon grated fresh
   ginger
Red curry satay sauce
   (pages 46–7)
560 g (1 lb 4 oz) tinned green
   jackfruit in brine, drained,
   rinsed and cut into chunks
200 g (7 oz) sweet potato,
   peeled and cut into chunks
400 ml (13½ fl oz) tinned
   coconut milk
185 ml (6 fl oz/¾ cup)
   vegetable stock
½–¾ teaspoon salt
1 small handful Thai basil
   leaves, chopped, plus extra
   to garnish
shredded coconut,
   to garnish
steamed brown rice,
   to serve

The jackfruit tree is a cousin of the fig and mulberry trees, native to South-East Asia. The ripe fruit tastes a bit like a magical cross between mango, pineapple and banana, but the unripe fruit makes an amazing meat substitute, with a texture that's not unlike shredded chicken or pork. Perfect for this tasty dish!

. . . .

Heat the oil in a medium saucepan over a medium heat. Add the onion and sauté for about 3 minutes, until soft. Add the garlic and ginger and cook, stirring, for 1 minute. Add the Red curry satay sauce, jackfruit and sweet potato and cook, stirring constantly, for about 3 minutes. Add the coconut milk, vegetable stock and salt. Bring to the boil, reduce the heat to medium–low and simmer for about 20 minutes, until the vegetables are cooked.

Remove from the heat, stir in the chopped basil leaves and garnish with the extra, along with the coconut. Serve with steamed rice.

NUTTY SPAGHETTI

Serves 2–3

1 teaspoon sesame oil
1 garlic clove, finely chopped
2 teaspoons finely chopped
   fresh ginger
60 g (2 oz/¼ cup) crunchy
   peanut butter
1 tablespoon soft
   brown sugar
1 tablespoon rice vinegar
50 g (1¾ oz/¼ cup) finely
   chopped tomatoes
140 g (5 oz) tomato paste
   (concentrated purée)
½ teaspoon chilli paste
   (or to taste)
½ bunch fresh basil leaves,
   finely chopped
170 g (6 oz) spaghetti
roasted tomatoes and wilted
   basil, to garnish

We told you we loved a fusion. This is a fun twist on the classic Italian tomato and basil pasta sauce, spiced up with ginger, sesame oil, rice vinegar and peanut butter.

. . . .

Heat the oil in a small saucepan over a medium heat. Add the garlic and ginger and cook, stirring, for about 1 minute, until just soft. Add 3 tablespoons of water along with the peanut butter, sugar, vinegar, tomatoes, tomato paste, chilli paste and chopped basil and cook, stirring frequently, for about 4 minutes, until the sauce is thick.

Meanwhile, cook the spaghetti according to the packet directions. Top the drained spaghetti with the sauce and garnish with the roasted tomatoes and wilted basil to serve.

VEGGIE NUT LOAF

Serves 4

3 tablespoons coconut oil
or oil of your choice
40 g (1½ oz/¼ cup) chopped
onion
360 g (12½ oz/4 cups) very
finely chopped
(or pulsed) mushrooms,
plus extra, sliced, to
decorate (optional)
2 teaspoons worcestershire
sauce
370 g (13 oz/2 cups) brown
lentils
3 garlic cloves, finely
chopped
1 teaspoon smoked paprika
½ teaspoon salt
½ teaspoon black pepper
3 eggs or egg substitute
125 g (4½ oz/½ cup) crunchy
peanut butter
120 g (4½ oz/1 cup) oat flour
tomato sauce (ketchup),
to glaze (optional)
green salad, to serve

We're bringing back nut roasts! They're packed with goodness and a perfect veg option for a festive meal or Sunday lunch, served with a simple green salad or with all the trimmings. Then slice up the leftovers the next day as part of a ploughman's lunch.

. . . .

Preheat the oven to 180°C (350°F) and line a 21 × 11 cm (8¼ × 4¼ in) loaf (bar) tin with baking paper.

Heat 2 tablespoons of the oil in a large frying pan over a medium heat and then sauté the onion until golden brown. Transfer the onion to a bowl and return the pan to the heat. Add another 1 tablespoon of oil and sauté the mushrooms with the worcestershire sauce until soft. Return the onion to the pan and add the lentils, garlic, paprika, salt and pepper. Cook, covered, for 4–5 minutes then remove from the heat and set aside to cool.

Pulse the cooled mushroom mixture with the eggs, peanut butter and oat flour in a food processor until mixed. Transfer to the prepared tin, smoothing the top with a spatula, and bake for 40–45 minutes, checking regularly, until a skewer inserted in the centre comes out clean. Halfway through the cooking time, top the loaf with extra mushrooms and glaze with tomato sauce if desired.

Cool in the tin for 10–15 minutes, then remove from the tin and cut into slices to serve alongside some salad.

WEST AFRICAN PEANUT SOUP

Serves 4–6

1.5 litres (51 fl oz/6 cups)
  vegetable broth
1 large red onion, chopped
3 tablespoons finely chopped
  fresh ginger
4 garlic cloves, finely chopped
1 teaspoon paprika
1 teaspoon salt
¼ teaspoon black pepper
200 g (7 oz) protein food
  (e.g. firm tofu, seitan,
  meat; optional)
125 g (3½ oz/½ cup) tomato
  paste (concentrated purée)
185 g (6½ oz/¾ cup)
  peanut butter
100 g (3½ oz/2 cups) finely
  chopped kale leaves, plus
  extra to garnish
chopped peanuts and hot sauce,
  to garnish
steamed brown rice, to serve
  (optional)

This is a simple version of the peanut soup or *mafé* that appears in various forms across West African countries such as Senegal, Gambia and Mali. It's a comforting and cosy winter meal, either on its own or over rice.

. . . .

Bring the stock to the boil in a large saucepan over a medium–high heat. Add the onion, ginger, garlic, paprika, salt, pepper and protein food, if using. Reduce the heat to medium–low and cook for 20 minutes. Add the tomato paste and simmer for 5–10 minutes. Add the peanut butter, increase the heat to medium and bring to the boil. Add the kale, then reduce the heat to medium–low and simmer, stirring frequently, for about 15 minutes.

Garnish with extra kale, chopped peanuts and hot sauce, and serve with rice if you wish.

PULLED JACKFRUIT BURGERS

Makes 8 burgers

8 burger buns
salad vegetables, coleslaw
   or Thai ginger salad
   (page 62), to serve

Pulled jackfruit
1 tablespoon oil
1 brown onion, chopped
560 g (1 lb 4 oz) green
   jackfruit in brine, drained
   and rinsed
Smoky barbecue satay sauce
   (pages 46–7)
1–2 tablespoons chilli paste
   (optional)

You'll never run out of uses for Smoky barbecue satay sauce. In fact, you might find it difficult to live without it, and these smoky barbecue meat-free burgers are only going to fuel that addiction. Warning: things are going to get messy, so make sure you've got two hands and plenty of napkins ready.

. . . .

Heat the oil in a large frying pan over a medium heat and cook the onion for about 5 minutes, until soft. Add 250 ml (8½ fl oz/1 cup) water, the jackfruit and Smoky barbecue satay sauce, and stir well. Reduce the heat to medium–low and cook, covered, for 20–25 minutes, stirring occasionally.

Preheat the oven to 200°C (400°F) and grease a baking tray or line it with baking paper.

Using a spatula, mash and pull the jackfruit into stringy strips so that it resembles pulled pork. Season with chilli paste, if using, and salt and pepper. Spread the pulled jackfruit evenly on the prepared tray and bake for 10–15 minutes, until golden brown. Toast the burger buns in the oven at the same time until golden brown. Fill the burger buns with the salad, top with jackfruit and serve.

PEANUT BUTTER

FOR MIDNIGHT

BRITTLE

Makes approximately 1 kg
(2 lb 3 oz) or 30 pieces

660 g (1 lb 7 oz/3 cups) sugar
125 g (4½ oz/½ cup) smooth
 peanut butter
1 teaspoon vanilla paste
 or natural extract
320 g (11½ oz/2 cups) roasted
 peanuts
1 teaspoon bicarbonate
 of soda (baking soda)

You may think brittle is an old-fashioned treat,
but why do you think it's been around for so long?
The shards of toffee can really be made with any
type of nuts, but (call us biased) we believe there's
a reason the peanut variety is such a mainstay. This
recipe is easiest if you use a sugar thermometer to
gauge when the toffee has cooked long enough.

Grease an 18 × 13 cm (7 × 5 in) baking tray or line
it with baking paper.

Combine the sugar with 125 ml (4 fl oz/½ cup) water
in a medium saucepan over a medium heat and
stir until the sugar has dissolved. Stir in the peanut
butter. Increase the heat to medium–high, and bring
to the boil, without stirring. You can occasionally
brush down the sides of the pan very gently using
a moist pastry brush.

When the sugar thermometer reaches 137°C (280°F),
stir in the vanilla and peanuts, taking care as the
mixture bubbles up. Continue cooking, stirring
constantly. When the sugar thermometer reaches
149°C (300°F), remove the pan from the heat and
stir in the bicarbonate of soda, taking care as the
mixture foams up.

Quickly and carefully pour onto the prepared baking
tray, immediately spread it out evenly using a silicone
spatula and score the surface using a knife. Once the
brittle has cooled completely, break it into pieces.

CLASSIC CUPS

Makes 10–12

255 g (9 oz) cooking
   chocolate of your choice
185 g (6½ oz/¾ cup) smooth
   or crunchy peanut butter
½ teaspoon natural vanilla
   extract
rice malt, coconut or maple
   syrup (optional)
Coconut salted caramel
   (pages 108–9, optional)
Quick and easy berry chia
   jam (page 27, optional)
small pretzels or other
   garnishes (optional)

These fan favourites are ridiculously easy to make at home. You probably have the three ingredients in your cupboard right now, so there's really no excuse to not walk straight into the kitchen and make a batch. Once you've mastered them, try adding an extra layer of flavour to the centres, such as salted caramel or jam. We've also got a pretzel-topped cup, but you could finish yours with some crunchy peanuts, dried raspberries or edible dried flowers before they set.

. . . .

Line a mini muffin tray with 10–12 mini baking cases, or sit the cases on a baking tray.

Melt two-thirds of the chocolate, either in a small bowl placed over a small saucepan of boiling water on the stovetop (the water must not touch the bowl) or in short bursts in the microwave.

Working one at a time, spoon 1 tablespoon of the melted chocolate into each paper case, tilting the case from side to side to spread the chocolate up the side to the desired height, ensuring there is an even chocolate base at the bottom of each cup. Set aside for 20 minutes to cool to room temperature or refrigerate for 5 minutes.

Meanwhile, in a separate bowl, mix the peanut butter with the vanilla and syrup, if using, to taste.

Using a teaspoon, fill each chocolate base with the peanut butter mixture, leaving a small chocolate gap at the top. If you would like to add an extra flavour, such as the Coconut salted caramel or Quick and easy berry chia jam, leave more of a gap with the peanut butter and then top with your next gooey layer.

Melt the remaining chocolate and, working one at a time, add a teaspoon or two over each cup. Rotate each cup from side to side to spread the chocolate evenly, ensuring it reaches the side. Top with a garnish, if using, then refrigerate for 20 minutes and serve. Leftover cups will keep in the refrigerator for up to 1 week or in the freezer for 1 year.

⟶ Pictured overleaf

CUP COOKIES

Makes 12

125 g (4½ oz/½ cup) unsalted
   butter or butter substitute,
   softened
95 g (3¼ oz/½ cup) soft
   brown sugar
110 g (4 oz/½ cup)
   white sugar
1 teaspoon natural
   vanilla extract
185 g (6½ oz/¾ cup) smooth
   or crunchy peanut butter
1 egg or egg substitute
225 g (8 oz/1½ cups) plain
   (all-purpose) flour
½ teaspoon bicarbonate of
   soda (baking soda)
12 frozen Classic cups
   (pages 92-3), paper
   cases removed

What happens if you take a home-made peanut
butter cup and place it in the centre of a
peanut butter cookie? Greatness – that's what
happens. You might want to make mini-sized cups
to use in these, or otherwise just make giant cookies
(no complaints here).

. . . .

Preheat the oven to 180°C (350°F) and line a baking
tray with baking paper.

Beat the butter and sugars in a medium bowl until
pale and fluffy. Add the vanilla, peanut butter and
egg, beating well after each addition. Sift the flour
with the bicarbonate of soda and fold into the butter
mixture until just smooth.

Using clean hands, roll tablespoons of the mixture
into balls, placing them about 3 cm (1¼ in) apart on
the prepared baking tray. Gently press each ball to
flatten slightly.

Bake for 10 minutes or until golden. Remove from the
oven and immediately place a chocolate cup gently
in the centre of each cookie. Leave the cookies on a
wire rack to cool completely, then store in an airtight
container in the refrigerator for up to 1 week.

PB+J DROP COOKIES

Makes 12

125 g (4½ oz/½ cup)
   peanut butter
2 tablespoons unsalted butter,
   melted and cooled
1 egg, lightly beaten, or egg
   substitute
60 ml (2 fl oz/¼ cup) syrup
   of your choice (maple, rice
   or coconut work best)
1 teaspoon natural vanilla
   extract
135 g (5 oz/1⅓ cups)
   almond meal
½ teaspoon baking powder
40 g (1½ oz/¼ cup)
   coconut sugar
¼ cup jam of your choice
   (see page 27 for Quick and
   easy berry chia jam)

How many ways can you PB+J? We say: there's no limit. Jam-drop cookies just like your nan made, but with a bit of extra nuttiness.

· ·

Line a baking tray with baking paper.

Combine the peanut butter, butter, egg, syrup and vanilla in a large bowl and stir until combined. Add the almond meal, baking powder and coconut sugar, then stir until the mixture forms a dough. Roll 1½ tablespoonfuls of dough into balls and place on the prepared tray, leaving about 3 cm (1¼ in) between them. Gently flatten each ball then push a clean thumb into the centre to make an indent for the jam. Refrigerate for 20–30 minutes.

Meanwhile, preheat the oven to 160°C (320°F).

Add ½ teaspoon of jam to the centre of each cookie. Bake for 15–20 minutes, until the edges of the cookies are golden brown. Cool on the tray on a wire rack, ensuring the jam is cooled completely before stacking or storing. The cookies will keep in an airtight container for up to 4 days.

BLISS BALLS

Makes 8–10

115 g (4 oz/⅓ cup) pure maple
   syrup or syrup of your choice
45 g (1½ oz/¼ cup) pitted
   dates, soaked in warm water
   for 20 minutes then drained

→ FOR ORIGINAL

250 g (9 oz/1 cup) peanut butter
45 g (1½ oz/⅓ cup)
   coconut flour
30 g (1 oz/¼ cup) unsweetened
   (Dutch) cocoa powder, plus
   extra to coat (optional)
40 g (1½ oz/¼ cup) finely chopped
   peanuts (optional)

→ FOR CHOC-CHIP

60 g (2 oz/¼ cup) peanut butter
50 g (1¾ oz/½ cup) rolled
   (porridge)oats
40 g (1½ oz/¼ cup) raw
   cashew nuts
½ teaspoon natural
   vanilla extract
45 g (1½ oz/¼ cup) dark chocolate
   chips or cacao nibs

Bliss balls are healthy, quick and easy to make: the perfect treat. Although we love a simple PB bliss ball (maybe rolled in crushed peanuts or cocoa powder), we're also partial to the choc-chip option (which includes bonus oats and cashews).

· ·

Line a baking tray with baking paper.

For the original bliss balls, pulse all the ingredients except the chopped peanuts (if using) in a food processor until thick. Using a large spoon or ice-cream scoop, drop even portions of the mixture onto the prepared baking tray. Refrigerate for 20–30 minutes, until somewhat firm. Using clean hands, roll into balls, then you can roll in the crushed peanuts for a crunchy coating or in extra cocoa powder.

For the choc-chip bliss balls, pulse all the ingredients except the chocolate chips in a food processor until combined but not sticky. Stir in the chocolate chips. Using clean hands, roll even portions of the mixture into balls.

Store in an airtight container in the refrigerator for up to 2 weeks.

FUDGE

Makes 10–12 pieces

180 g (6½ oz/2 cups)
  desiccated (shredded)
  coconut
250 g (9 oz/1 cup) smooth
  peanut butter
125 ml (4 fl oz/½ cup) coconut
  oil, melted
3–5 tablespoons coconut
  nectar or maple syrup
pinch of sea salt
1 teaspoon natural vanilla
  extract

A creamy and naturally sweet craving fix. You can't just stop at one piece, trust us!

· ·

Line a 20 × 10 cm (8 × 4 in) loaf (bar) tin with baking paper.

Process the desiccated coconut in a food processor on high until it forms a creamy butter, about 4 minutes. Scrape down the side as needed.

Add the peanut butter and coconut oil and process once more. Add the nectar or syrup 1 tablespoon at a time, until the mixture reaches your desired sweetness. Add the sea salt and vanilla and process once more.

Transfer to the prepared tin and spread evenly using a spatula. Cover and refrigerate for 20–30 minutes until set. Store in an airtight container in the refrigerator for up to 2 weeks.

GROWN-UP TRUFFLES

Makes 16–20

½ teaspoon coconut oil
150 g (5½ oz/1 cup) dark, milk and/or white chocolate melts (buttons), plus extra to decorate
¼ teaspoon sea salt
peanut butter or unsweetened (Dutch) cocoa powder (optional), to decorate

Filling

185 g (6½ oz/¾ cup) peanut butter
125 ml (4 fl oz/½ cup) rice malt syrup or syrup of your choice
⅛ teaspoon sea salt
35 g (1¼ oz/¼ cup) coconut flour
40 g (1½ oz/1⅓ cups) puffed rice cereal

Bring out your inner artist by decorating these treats with a drizzle of contrasting chocolate colour or extra PB. This might sound like an activity children would enjoy, but we seriously encourage you to hide these from any children in your life. Instead, serve them with an after-dinner cocktail (see pages 126–27 for ideas) or eat them all yourself. Maybe in bed.

. . . .

To make the filling, line a baking tray with baking paper. Using a food processor or electric mixer, beat the peanut butter, syrup and salt. Add the coconut flour slowly, stopping when the mixture is no longer wet but not very dry. Fold through the puffed rice cereal. Roll tablespoons of the mixture into balls and sit them on the prepared tin. Freeze for 5 minutes to chill slightly.

Melt the coconut oil and chocolate together in a bowl placed over a saucepan of boiling water on the stovetop (the water must not touch the bowl) or in short bursts in the microwave. Stir in the salt.

Using a fork, dip the peanut butter balls one at a time in the chocolate and use a spoon to ensure they are covered. Return them to the baking tray. Decorate, then freeze or refrigerate until the chocolate coating is set. Store with baking paper between layers in an airtight container in the refrigerator for 1–2 weeks.

NICE-CREAM SUNDAES

Serves 2–3

1 quantity Coconut salted
  caramel (pages 108–9),
  to serve
crushed roasted peanuts
  or Brittle (page 90),
  to garnish

Banana nice cream
3 large frozen ripe bananas
  (see page 28)
60 g (2 oz/¼ cup) peanut
  butter
60 ml (2 fl oz/¼ cup) coconut
  cream
¼ teaspoon natural vanilla
  extract
⅛ teaspoon ground cinnamon
⅛ teaspoon sea salt

In the running for best peanut butter flavour partners, we already have some good contenders (jam, chocolate, apple …) but banana makes a pretty good case. Elvis Presley was said to be partial to a peanut butter and banana sandwich, so perhaps the King would have enjoyed this banana nice-cream sundae. Nice cream is easy to whip up whenever you're feeling like something sweet, and it goes well with all your favourite toppings.

. . . .

If you prefer to serve the Coconut salted caramel warm, heat through gently and set aside to cool slightly.

To make the nice cream, blend the bananas in a food processor or high-speed blender until smooth and creamy, scraping the sides if needed. Add the remaining ingredients and pulse briefly to just incorporate. Place in the freezer for a minute or two to firm up, then serve immediately, topped with the Coconut salted caramel sauce and garnished with the peanuts or brittle.

SALTED CARAMEL CHEESECAKE

Serves 12–14

peanuts, whole or finely chopped, and edible flowers, to garnish

Crust
185 g (6½ oz) mildly sweet biscuits (e.g. graham crackers, Granitas, digestives)
75 g (2¾ oz) unsalted butter, melted, or 75 ml (2½ fl oz) coconut oil
75 g (2¾ oz/⅓ cup) sugar

Filling
400 ml (13½ fl oz) tinned full-fat coconut cream
155 g (5½ oz/1 cup) raw cashew nuts, soaked in water for at least 6 hours or overnight and drained
135 g (5 oz/¾ cup) pitted dates, soaked in water for at least 6 hours or overnight and drained
½ teaspoon sea salt
90 g (3 oz/⅓ cup) smooth peanut butter

Did you know that people in the Netherlands call peanut butter *pindakaas*, which literally means 'peanut cheese'? We're not entirely sure if that sounds disgusting or delicious, but we are sure that peanut cheese*cake* is most definitely delicious, especially with the addition of salted caramel. This recipe is actually made with coconut cream, instead of the usual cream cheese. It has a few different elements but it's absolutely worth it – we're sure of that too.

. . . .

Grease a 25 cm (10 in) springform tin and line the bottom with baking paper.

To make the crust, crush the biscuits to crumbs in a food processor or blender. Transfer to a large bowl and mix with the butter and sugar. The mixture will be thick and sandy. Press firmly into the prepared tin, covering the bottom and a little way up the side. Refrigerate for 2 hours.

To make the filling, pulse all the ingredients in a food processor until smooth, scraping down the side as needed. Pour the filling over the chilled crust. Gently tap the tin on the work surface a few times. Freeze for 1½–2 hours, until set.

Meanwhile, prepare the salted caramel. Combine the coconut cream, coconut sugar and salt in a medium saucepan over a medium–high heat. Bring to the boil, watching carefully to ensure it doesn't boil over, then immediately reduce the temperature to low and

Coconut salted caramel

400 ml (13½ fl oz) tinned
  full-fat coconut cream
80 g (2¾ oz/½ cup) coconut
  sugar
⅛ teaspoon sea salt
1 teaspoon coconut oil
1 teaspoon natural
  vanilla extract

simmer gently for 20–25 minutes, stirring occasionally. Now begin to stir more frequently, to incorporate the darker caramel bits from the bottom, until the sauce is a dark amber colour and is thick enough to coat the back of a spoon, 10–15 minutes. Remove from the heat and stir in the coconut oil and vanilla extract. Refrigerate for 1 hour.

Pour as much of the salted caramel sauce over the set filling as desired, then gently tap the tin on the work surface a few times to even out the caramel layer. Return to the freezer for another 20–30 minutes, until the caramel layer has set, then garnish with peanuts and edible flowers to serve. The leftovers will keep in an airtight container in the refrigerator for up to 5 days.

⟶ Pictured page 110

SAUCY CHOCOLATE BROWNIES

Makes about 12

125 g (4½ oz/½ cup) peanut butter, plus extra to serve

1 banana

6 pitted dates

125 ml (4 fl oz/½ cup) maple syrup

1 teaspoon natural vanilla extract

75 g (2¾ oz/½ cup) plain (all-purpose) flour or gluten-free flour of your choice

55 g (2 oz/½ cup) almond meal

60 g (2 oz/½ cup) cacao powder or unsweetened (Dutch) cocoa powder

½ teaspoon bicarbonate of soda (baking soda)

1 teaspoon baking powder

175 g (6 oz/1 cup) dark chocolate chips and/or cacao nibs

PB brownie plus salted dark chocolate PB sauce equals an extra indulgent dessert. As usual, mix things up. Why not try this with a scoop of Banana nice cream (page 107)? Or use the sauce in a milkshake or smoothie (pages 122–23)? Or perhaps lose the sauce altogether and instead cover your brownie with Quick and easy berry chia jam (page 27) or Coconut salted caramel (pages 108–9)? Whichever way you take things, you can feel pretty confident that the result is going to be good.

. . . .

To make the Salted dark chocolate sauce, melt the chocolate in a small bowl placed over a small saucepan of boiling water on the stovetop (the water must not touch the bowl), stirring occasionally, or in short bursts in the microwave. Add the peanut butter, syrup and salt and stir thoroughly.

Remove from the heat and gradually stir in the milk until the sauce reaches the desired consistency.

Preheat the oven to 175°C (345°F) and grease a 28 × 18 cm (11 × 7 in) tin.

In a food processor, combine the peanut butter, banana, dates, syrup and vanilla until smooth. In a separate large bowl, combine the flour, almond meal, cacao powder, bicarbonate of soda, baking powder and a pinch of salt. Pour the peanut butter mixture into the flour mixture and mix thoroughly. Pour into the prepared tin and top with the chocolate chips.

Salted dark chocolate sauce

50 g (1¾ oz) dark chocolate
  (70% cocoa)

3 tablespoons peanut butter

2 tablespoons syrup of your choice
  (e.g. rice malt, coconut, maple)

¼ teaspoon salt

75 ml (2½ fl oz) milk of your choice

Bake for about 30 minutes, checking regularly after 20 minutes, until a skewer inserted in the centre comes out clean.

Cool completely in the tin before cutting, and serve topped with the salted dark chocolate sauce and extra peanut butter.

← Pictured page 111

NICE-CREAM SANDWICH

Makes 9–12

Banana nice cream (page 107)
Quick and easy berry chia
  jam (page 27), Salted dark
  chocolate sauce (pages
  112–13) or Coconut salted
  caramel (pages 108–9)
  (optional)

Peanut butter cookies
115 g (4 oz/½ cup) caster
  (superfine) sugar
115 g (4 oz/½ cup) firmly
  packed soft brown sugar
1 teaspoon bicarbonate of soda
  (baking soda)
¼ teaspoon salt
250 g (9 oz/1 cup) unsalted
  butter or butter substitute,
  softened
2 large eggs, lightly beaten,
  or egg substitute
75 g (2¾ oz/½ cup) plain
  (all-purpose) flour
200 g (7 oz) peanut butter,
  softened
chocolate chips or cacao nibs
  (optional)

Make a batch of Peanut butter cookies so you can transform your nice cream into a summer nice-cream sandwich. These cookies are also delicious sandwiched with Peanut butter frosting (page 117), or just on their own. You can make up the cookie dough ahead of time and freeze in balls to bake whenever you please – just make sure the cookies are totally cool before you start your sandwich making.

. . . .

Preheat the oven to 175°C (345°F) and line two baking trays with baking paper.

To make the cookies, combine the sugars, bicarbonate of soda and salt in a large bowl. Add the butter and eggs and mix well. Gradually fold in the sifted flour. Add the peanut butter and mix well. Stir in the chocolate chips. Roll tablespoonfuls of the mixture into balls and arrange on the prepared tray, about 3 cm (1¼ in) apart.

If you prefer soft cookies, refrigerate the dough for at least 1 hour. Bake for 10–15 minutes. Transfer to a wire rack to cool.

To make the cookie sandwiches, place a large scoop of nice cream on the underside of a cookie, and top with a layer of jam or sauce if you wish. Place another cookie on top and press gently. Repeat until all the cookies have been used. Place in the freezer to firm up for 20 minutes, then serve immediately.

CUPCAKES

Makes 12–14

185 g (6½ oz/1¼ cups) plain
  (all-purpose) flour
145 g (5 oz/⅔ cup) caster
  (superfine) sugar
1 tablespoon baking powder
125 ml (4 fl oz/½ cup) milk of
  your choice
2 eggs, lightly whisked,
  or egg substitute
125 g (4½ oz/½ cup) unsalted
  butter or butter substitute,
  softened
2 teaspoons vanilla bean paste
  or natural extract
200 g (7 oz) smooth
  peanut butter

Peanut butter frosting
250 g (9 oz/1 cup) unsalted
  butter or butter substitute,
  softened
250 g (9 oz/1 cup) peanut butter
375 g (13 oz/3 cups) icing
  (confectioners') sugar
1 teaspoon natural vanilla extract
½ teaspoon salt
2 tablespoons milk of your choice

Is there anything more satisfying than a perfect swirl of PB frosting on top of a cupcake? These are NYC-worthy. Go nuts with the extra toppings: we've used crushed Brittle (page 90), freeze-dried raspberries, chocolate shavings, cocoa powder and, of course, extra peanut butter.

· · · · · · · · · · · · · · · · · · · ·

Preheat the oven to 180°C (350°F) and line a muffin tin with paper cases.

Whisk the dry ingredients with a pinch of salt in a large bowl. Beat the milk, eggs, butter and vanilla until pale and fluffy. Slowly add the peanut butter and continue beating until the mixture is smooth. Slowly add the dry mixture until the ingredients are combined.

Spoon into the prepared tin and bake for 15–20 minutes, or until a skewer inserted into the centre of a cupcake comes out clean. Cool the cupcakes in the tin on a wire rack.

Meanwhile, make the frosting. Beat the butter and peanut butter in a large bowl until creamy. Slowly fold in the sugar until completely combined. Stir in the vanilla and salt, then fold in the milk until completely combined. Place in the refrigerator to set.

Remove the cupcakes from the tin and sit on the wire rack. Top with the frosting, using either a knife or a piping (icing) bag with a fluted tip, then have fun adding any extra toppings.

PB+J LAMINGTONS

Makes 12–15

120 g (4½ oz) unsalted butter
or butter substitute, softened
115 g (4 oz/½ cup) caster
(superfine) sugar
1 teaspoon natural vanilla extract
150 ml (5 fl oz) milk of
your choice
2 eggs or egg substitute
225 g (8 oz/1½ cups)
self-raising flour
30 g (1 oz/¼ cup) cornflour
(cornstarch)
200 g (7 oz) desiccated
(shredded) coconut
60 g (2 oz/¼ cup) smooth
peanut butter, softened
60 g (2 oz/¼ cup) jam of
your choice

Icing

375 g (13 oz/3 cups) icing
(confectioners') sugar
40 g (1½ oz/⅓ cup)
unsweetened (Dutch)
cocoa powder
80 ml (2½ fl oz/⅓ cup) milk
of your choice
2 tablespoons melted unsalted
butter or butter substitute

An American take on an Aussie classic: an ooey-gooey peanut-butter-and-jam centre sandwiched between chocolate-and-coconut-covered sponge.

· ·

Preheat the oven to 180°C (350°F) and line a 23 × 13 cm (9 × 5 in) loaf (bar) tin with baking paper.

Whisk together the butter, sugar, vanilla, milk, eggs and a pinch of salt in a large bowl. Add the flour and cornflour and whisk to form a smooth batter. Pour into the prepared tin and bake for about 20 minutes, until a skewer inserted into the centre comes out clean. Cool in the tin for 5 minutes, then turn onto a wire rack to cool completely.

Meanwhile, make the chocolate icing by whisking all the ingredients together with a pinch of salt and ½ tablespoon of hot water. Fill a wide bowl or baking tin with desiccated coconut.

Slice the sponge into 6–8 squares and refrigerate for 15–20 minutes. Then, working one square at a time, dip each sponge in the icing to coat completely, then roll immediately in the desiccated coconut. Place the dipped squares in the freezer for 1–2 hours to firm up.

Remove the sponge squares from the freezer and cut each in half crossways using a large serrated knife. Carefully spread jam on one cut side and peanut butter on the other. Sandwich the two layers together with jam and peanut butter facing. Store in an airtight container in the refrigerator for up to 5 days.

PEANUT BUTTER

FOR DRINKS

FOR MILKSHAKES START WITH

2–4 ice cubes · 125 ml (4 fl oz/½ cup) milk of your choice

60 g (2 oz/¼ cup) peanut butter

WHAT'S YOUR FLAVOUR?

CHOCOLATE PRETZEL

2 scoops chocolate frozen yoghurt or chocolate ice cream

pretzels, whole and crushed, to garnish

Salted dark chocolate sauce (pages 112–13), to garnish

COCONUT SALTED CARAMEL

2 scoops vanilla frozen yoghurt or vanilla ice cream

3 tablespoons Coconut salted caramel (pages 108–9), plus 1 tablespoon extra, to garnish

PB+J

2 scoops strawberry frozen yoghurt or strawberry ice cream

Quick and easy berry chia jam (page 27) and fresh strawberries, to garnish

THEN WHAT?

FOR SMOOTHIES START WITH

4–6 ice cubes · 60 ml (2 fl oz/¼ cup) milk of your choice

2 frozen bananas (see page 28) · 60 g (2 oz/¼ cup) peanut butter

WHAT'S YOUR FLAVOUR?

ORIGINAL

crushed peanuts or
Brittle (page 90),
to garnish

BERRY

150 g (5½ oz/1 cup) frozen berries

berry jam and edible flowers,
to garnish

CHOCOLATE ESPRESSO

2 teaspoons cacao powder or unsweetened
(Dutch) cocoa powder

30 ml (1 fl oz) espresso or black coffee of your choice

coffee beans and dried fruit, to garnish

Whiz all the ingredients in a high-speed blender until smooth.
Pour into a glass, top with the garnishes and enjoy!

Each serves 2; milkshakes pictured page 124, smoothies page 125

COCKTAILS

Each serves 1

If you want recipes for kids, that's the next chapter. This is one page that is definitely all about our grown-up peanut butter nutters. Smooth PB gives the ultimate twist to some bar favourites: a bitter-orange Negroni, party-starting Espresso martini and creamy Alexander.

Double straining involves using both a cocktail strainer and a fine-mesh sieve to make sure you get a perfectly smooth sip. And you can make your own sugar syrup easily enough by dissolving 2 parts sugar in 1 part water in a saucepan over a low heat. Keep it in the refrigerator, ready to sweeten up your next party drinks.

. . . .

Combine all the ingredients in a cocktail shaker, shake with ice cubes, double strain into a glass and top with the garnish.

⟶ Pictured overleaf

ESPRESSO MARTINI

½ teaspoon unsalted
smooth peanut butter

30 ml (1 fl oz) espresso coffee

30 ml (1 fl oz) gin or vodka

30 ml (1 fl oz) coffee liqueur

10 ml (¼ fl oz) sugar syrup (see opposite)

coffee beans, to garnish

NEGRONI

4 drops peanut oil

¼ teaspoon unsalted
smooth peanut butter

20 ml (¾ fl oz) gin

20 ml (¾ fl oz) sweet vermouth

20 ml (¾ fl oz) Campari

extra ice cubes and thinly sliced orange
(fresh or dried), to garnish

ALEXANDER

½ teaspoon unsalted
smooth peanut butter

30 ml (1 fl oz) macadamia liqueur

30 ml (1 fl oz) white crème de cacao

30 ml (1 fl oz) coconut cream shaken
with 1 teaspoon egg white or egg white
substitute, to garnish

PEANUT BUTTER

FOR KIDS

PB+J SUSHI

Makes 6

2 slices bread of your choice,
   crusts cut off
2 tablespoons peanut butter
3 tablespoons jam of your
   choice

This is ideal for when you're munching away on some Red curry sushi (page 55) and there's a little person who wants to get in on the fun. You could add a layer of mashed banana or grated coconut for extra flavour. It's also great in lunchboxes, but make sure to check if your school or organisation has a food-allergy policy before packing any PB treats.

· ·

Lightly spread each bread slice with peanut butter. Gently add a layer of jam over the peanut butter.

Carefully roll up each bread slice, then cut each roll into three pieces.

SNACK ATTACK!
IDEAS FOR LITTLE PB FANS

PB + CELERY + RAISINS

PB + STRAWBERRY

PB + DATE + CACAO NIBS

PB + AVOCADO

CAULIFLOWER BUFFALO WINGS

Serves 2–3

2 teaspoons coconut oil
  or oil of your choice
60 g (2 oz/¼ cup) crunchy
  peanut butter
60 ml (2 fl oz/¼ cup) milk
  of your choice
45 g (1½ oz/¼ cup) rice flour
  or flour of your choice
2 tablespoons honey
  or coconut syrup
2 tablespoons water
1 teaspoon vinegar
½ teaspoon sea salt
90 g (3 oz/1½ cups) Japanese
  (panko) breadcrumbs
40 g (1½ oz/¼ cup) finely
  chopped peanuts
1 head cauliflower
chopped vegetables and
  sauces, to serve

These crunchy 'wings' are most certainly going to become part of your regular family dinner rotation, and good thing too, because PB is full of things that are great for growing bodies. Continue the crunch (and the cutlery-free zone) with a pile of chopped fresh veggies. Panko breadcrumbs can be found in the international section of most grocery stores.

. . . .

Preheat the oven to 190°C (375°F) and line a large baking tray with baking paper.

In a large bowl or food processor, mix the oil, peanut butter, milk, rice flour, honey, water, vinegar and salt until smooth.

Mix the breadcrumbs and peanuts in a medium bowl.

Separate the cauliflower into small florets. Working one at a time, dip each floret into the peanut butter mixture to coat completely, then roll in the breadcrumb mixture to coat. Place on the prepared baking tray, leaving a small gap between them.

Bake for 25–30 minutes, turning at least once, until golden brown.

Serve immediately with a handful of veggies and your child's favourite sauce.

CRISPY RICE TREATS

Makes about 12

135 g (5 oz) smooth
    peanut butter
165 ml (5½ fl oz) maple
    or rice malt syrup
1 teaspoon natural
    vanilla extract
150 g (5½ oz/5 cups)
    puffed rice cereal
melted chocolate and
    crushed peanuts,
    to garnish (optional)

Tim practically grew up on these simple snacks. We know this is meant to be a chapter for kids, but good luck keeping these out of adult hands (especially if you go and top them with some melted chocolate and crushed peanuts).

. . . .

Line a 28 × 18 cm (11 × 7 in) baking tin with baking paper.

Combine the peanut butter, syrup and vanilla in a microwave-safe bowl or small saucepan. Heat the bowl slowly in the microwave or the saucepan on the stovetop until the mixture forms a creamy sauce. Set aside to cool for 10 minutes.

Place the rice cereal in a large bowl, pour over the cooled sauce and mix gently until well combined.

Spoon into the prepared baking tin, smoothing the top with a spatula or the back of a spoon. Refrigerate until set, about 40 minutes. Cut into squares to serve, perhaps topped with some melted chocolate or crushed peanuts. The treats will keep in an airtight container in the refrigerator for up to 1 week.

BANANA BITES

Makes about 18

3 bananas
125 g (4½ oz/½ cup) crunchy
   peanut butter
150 g (5½ oz) chocolate
   chips or cooking chocolate,
   broken into pieces

These cold, chocolate-y bites look almost as great as they taste and are a guaranteed crowd-pleaser at birthday parties – just remember to check for allergies.

· ·

Line a baking tray with baking paper.

Cut the bananas into slices 2 cm (¾ in) thick. Spoon ½–1 tablespoon of peanut butter onto a banana slice, then top with a second banana slice. Place on the prepared baking tray and repeat with the remaining banana slices. Freeze for 1 hour.

Melt the chocolate, either in a small bowl placed over a small saucepan of boiling water on the stovetop (the water must not touch the bowl) or in short bursts in the microwave. Dip half of each banana sandwich in the chocolate. Return to the baking tray and freeze for 20–30 minutes before serving.

These will keep in an airtight container in the refrigerator for 2 days or in the freezer for up to 2 weeks.

YOGHURT POPS

Makes 8

4 large bananas, cut
   into chunks
500 g (1 lb 2 oz/2 cups)
   vanilla coconut yoghurt
   or yoghurt of your choice
125 g (4½ oz/½ cup) smooth
   peanut butter
110 g (4 oz/½ cup) mixed
   berries

Again, we're saying these are 'for kids'. Yes, they're perfect for a day spent running through sprinklers and reapplying sunblock, but they're also perfect for a grown-up day spent lounging on pool floats and reading trashy novels. You'll need iceblock (popsicle/ ice lolly) moulds and sticks for this recipe, which you can find at most home or variety shops.

· ·

Blend the bananas, yoghurt and peanut butter in a blender or food processor until smooth and set aside. Separately, blend the berries until smooth.

Divide half the banana mixture between iceblock (popsicle/ice lolly) moulds – they should be about a third full. Place in the freezer for 15 minutes. Next top the moulds with the berry mixture and return them to the freezer for an additional 15 minutes. Finally, fill the remaining third of the moulds with the rest of the banana mixture. Push sticks into each mould and return them to the freezer for 45 minutes.

Once the pops are completely frozen, briefly run the moulds under the tap, then gently pull each pop out of its mould by the stick and enjoy immediately. These will keep in the freezer for up to 1 month.

PEANUT BUTTER

FOR DOGS

DOG PB

Makes approximately
370 g (13 oz)

370 g (13 oz/1⅓ cups)
  unsalted roasted peanuts
olive oil (optional)
1 teaspoon brewer's yeast
1 teaspoon chia seeds
1 teaspoon linseeds
  (flax seeds)

Frankie says: 'Store-bought peanut butter can be dangerous for me because it might contain xylitol, a common sweetener that is poisonous to dogs. But my vet says peanuts are a great source of healthy fats, proteins and vitamins, so my humans made a natural peanut butter especially for me! After all, I don't want human germs all over my jar. Dog PB has some added chia, linseed and brewer's yeast to keep my skin and coat healthy and shiny. A toy filled with DPB will keep me entertained for hours, and apparently a spoonful of DPB is a great way to sneak me tablets, but I wouldn't know.' On a practical note, see page 9 for how to sterilise your storage jars.

. . . .

Pulse the peanuts in a food processor until smooth. If the nuts turn into a dry paste, continue processing and add olive oil in a slow stream until the mixture is smooth.

Transfer the peanut butter to a bowl and thoroughly mix in the remaining ingredients. Spoon into sterilised jars and store in a cool, dry place for up to 6 months.

DOG BISCUITS

Makes approximately 30

150 g (5½ oz/1 cup) wholemeal
  (whole-wheat) flour
1 teaspoon chia seeds
1 teaspoon linseeds
  (flax seeds)
125 g (4½ oz/½ cup)
  home-made or xylitol-free
  peanut butter
60 g (2 oz/¼ cup) mashed ripe
  banana
60 ml (2 fl oz/¼ cup) stock,
  bone broth or water
bone-shaped cookie cutter

It's always good to give your dog a bikkie that you could eat yourself – you know, if you were into that banana and beef stock flavour combo. Another reminder to only use home-made PB for your dog, or to make sure your peanut butter contains no xylitol. Any stock used should also be low in sodium and free from onion or garlic – as usual, home-made is best!

Preheat the oven to 180°C (350°F) and line a baking tray with baking paper.

Combine the flour, chia seeds, linseeds, peanut butter and banana in a large mixing bowl. Add the stock and stir until well combined. The dough should be thick.

Using clean hands, press the dough into a ball. Place on a lightly floured work surface and roll to about 5 mm (¼ in) thick using a rolling pin. Cut the dough into biscuits using a cookie cutter and arrange on the prepared baking sheet.

Bake for 15–20 minutes, or until golden brown. Cool on the tray, then store in an airtight container for up to 6 weeks.

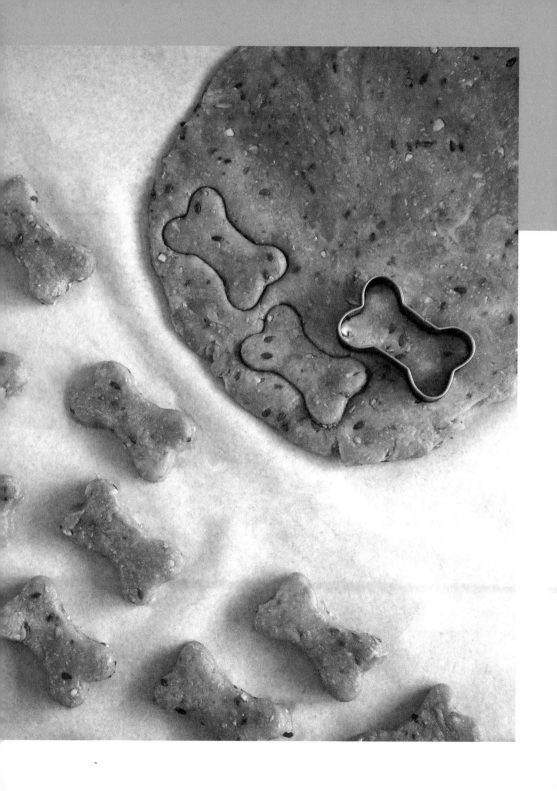

PUPSICLES

Makes 6

2 large bananas
125 ml (4½ fl oz/½ cup) stock,
  bone broth or water
60 g (2 oz/¼ cup)
  home-made or
  xylitol-free peanut butter
½ teaspoon chia seeds
½ teaspoon linseeds
  (flax seeds)
6 dog chew sticks

When it's sweltering hot and you're enjoying your Yoghurt pop (page 143), it's only fair that your furry friend has something cooling and delicious as well. We'll say it again: please remember to only use home-made PB for your dog, otherwise find a peanut butter with no added xylitol, and stock for dogs needs to be low in sodium and free from onion or garlic.

. . . .

Blend all the ingredients except the chew sticks in a food processor or blender until smooth. Pour into ice-cube trays and freeze for 20–30 minutes, until the mixture is firm enough to hold the chew stick upright when inserted. Insert all the sticks and return the trays to the freezer until completely frozen. Store in the freezer for up to 1 month.

JAMES, TIM + FRANKIE WOULD LIKE TO THANK ...

Kate Berry (@hellokateberry) for the photography and food styling that brought our ideas to life.

Annie Brady (@mypurposefulpantry) and Vicki Veranese of Alive and Wild (@livingliveraw) for the helping hand in the kitchen.

Mr Jason Grant (@mrjasongrant) for his beautiful props and styling assistance.

Surface Society (@surfacesociety) for the awesome tiles.

Ashley McLaughlin (@edible_perspective) for the perfect cover shot.

Aimee Carruthers (@carruthersandco) for taking our aesthetic and turning it into this amazing design.

The Hardie Grant team (@hardiegrantbooks), especially Emily Hart and Jane Willson.

And our customers at The Byron Bay Peanut Butter Co. (@byronbaypeanutbutter) for making our dream of making peanut butter in paradise a reality.

FIND A RECIPE

Published in 2020 by Hardie Grant Books,
an imprint of Hardie Grant Publishing

Hardie Grant Books (Melbourne)
Building 1, 658 Church Street
Richmond, Victoria 3121

Hardie Grant Books (London)
5th & 6th Floors
52–54 Southwark Street
London SE1 1UN

hardiegrantbooks.com

A catalogue record for this
book is available from the
National Library of Australia

Peanut Butter: Breakfast, Lunch, Dinner, Midnight
ISBN 978 1 74379 575 0

10 9 8 7 6 5 4 3 2 1

Publishing Director: Jane Willson
Project Editor: Emily Hart
Editor: Nicola Young
Design Manager: Jessica Lowe
Designer: Aimee Carruthers
Production Manager: Todd Rechner

Printed in China by Leo Paper Products LTD.
Colour reproduction by Splitting Image Colour Studio

This book uses 15 ml (½ fl oz) tablespoons; cooks with
20 ml (¾ fl oz) tablespoons should be scant with their
tablespoon measurements.